The Exciting S
Barcelona

Rob Waring, *Series Editor*

HEINLE
CENGAGE Learning

Australia • Brazil • Japan • Korea • Mexico • Singapore • Spain • United Kingdom • United States

Words to Know

This story is set in Catalonia, Spain, in the city of Barcelona [bɑːˈsəloʊnə]. It takes place on a busy street called the Ramblas [rɑːmblɑːs], which is in the centre of the city.

Catalonia

Barcelona

EUROPE

SPAIN

Mediterranean Sea

AFRICA

N W E S

(A) Barcelona. Read the paragraph. Then complete the sentences with the correct form of the underlined words.

Barcelona is famous for its active street life, particularly the entertainers on the Ramblas, a pedestrian-only avenue in the centre of the city. The Ramblas is full of musicians and actors who are able to express themselves very artistically. They often give spontaneous performances on the streets, starting to perform with any group that may be nearby. They frequently improvise and involve spectators in their shows. These entertainers, who come from all over the world, provide a stimulating environment for Barcelona's residents and visitors.

1. A _____ activity is one that is not planned, but decided upon suddenly.
2. A _____ is someone who travels on foot.
3. When something is _____ , it is inspiring and exciting.
4. To _____ is to create and perform without preparation or practice.
5. To express oneself _____ means to allow one's creativity to flow freely.

onlookers

make-up

B Street Entertainers. Read the definitions. Then complete the paragraph with the correct forms of the words.

dais: a platform that is higher than the ground around it
gangster: a member of an organised group of criminals
make-up: a coloured substance usually put on the face to enhance or change appearance
market stalls: small shops that sell items on the street
onlooker: someone who is observing something; a spectator

Surrounded by shoppers and busy (1)_____, there are several types of interesting entertainers in Barcelona. One popular type is the human statue, a person who dresses up as a famous character, such as a (2)_____, and stands perfectly still like a statue. Other performers wear costumes or cover their faces with (3)_____ before dancing around. Musicians stand in the street or on a small (4)_____ while they play entertaining music. The (5)_____ are often amazed, and sometimes shocked, as they explore the streets around the Ramblas.

market stalls

a gangster human statue

Life on the Ramblas

dais

3

When walking through the centre of Barcelona, Spain, one is surrounded by the sights and sounds of entertainers expressing themselves artistically: musicians playing jazz in the street, costumed dancers moving to the beat, living statues, street theatre or entertainers putting on an **impromptu**[1] show for the public. The unique and dynamic atmosphere of this Mediterranean city makes visitors feel like they are attending a party that never ends.

Residents of the city, as well as tourists, love Barcelona because it has a lively and friendly feel each time one walks down the street. 'There's something very special about Barcelona,' says one resident who really loves the welcoming atmosphere. 'Anytime you go out of your house there's always something going on. You'll always find a friend on the streets. It's where [the people live]. You're not in your place, you're on the street.' Apparently, some of the most exciting things in Barcelona happen in the streets of the city, that's why some of its residents don't waste their time at home. But how do these events occur? Who plans them? The Barcelona resident further explains, 'Things happen, but they're not organised.' He then offers an example by indicating a group performing nearby, 'Like this group ... the circus group, they're just doing it on their own. Mixing with this group of jazz musicians and [they] just do it – improvising.'

---

[1]**impromptu:** not planned in advance

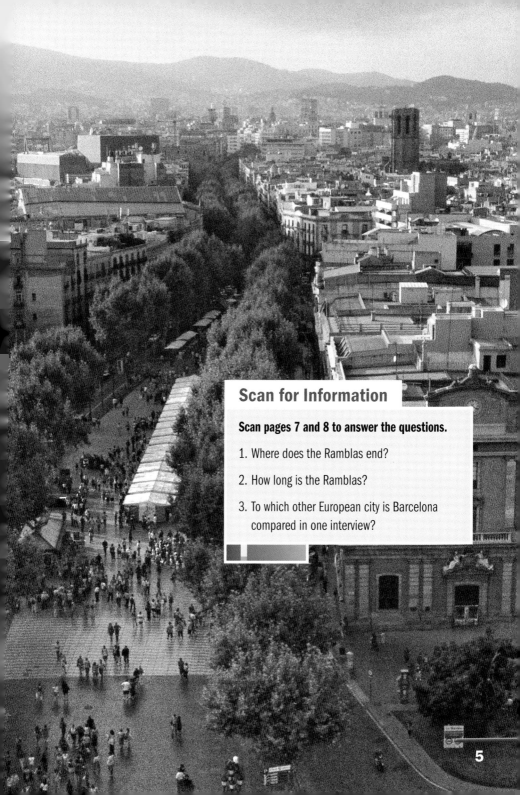

Scan for Information

Scan pages 7 and 8 to answer the questions.

1. Where does the Ramblas end?

2. How long is the Ramblas?

3. To which other European city is Barcelona compared in one interview?

Winding through the very heart of Barcelona, the Ramblas is the central point of all of this innovative activity. It's the wide, pedestrian-only **boulevard**[2] that cuts right through the middle of the Catalan city and ends at the harbour. The Ramblas is one of the most famous streets in town; it's well known by both locals and those just visiting Barcelona. Lined with trees, cafés, and market stalls, it often serves as a visitor highlight and a social **hub**[3] of the city, used as a meeting place for people of all ages.

There is so much to see on the three-quarter-mile-long Ramblas: musicians, artists and many other kinds of entertainers. Some of these performers are just improvising their acts in the street and involving everyone – young and old. At other times they complement one another and play together. Couples dance together, children play and older men and women dance traditional dances in a circle. It's an intense place, and people from all over the world often gather here to enjoy the atmosphere.

---

[2]**boulevard:** a tree-lined avenue
[3]**hub:** central point

Of course other lively and interesting streets exist in European cities, but what differentiates the Ramblas Is that it is full of life at almost any time of the day; it seems to never sleep. One artist, who was previously in Amsterdam but who now works on the Ramblas, compares Barcelona **favourably**[4] to the Dutch city. He explains: 'You can go out in the street at night and it's always lively. It's never "nobody [is] in the Ramblas," for example. There's always – every hour [of every] day – there's life.'

As the artist continues to speak, it becomes obvious that for this contented resident, time spent in Barcelona has been a positive experience. '[When] I came here I felt somehow better than in Amsterdam,' he explains. '[I felt] more alive ... more *vital*.[5] That makes it very enjoyable, at least for me, and inspiring too.'

---

[4]**favourably:** in a positive manner
[5]*vital* [vaɪtəl]: Spanish word for energetic and healthy; in English 'vital' [viːtɑːl]

Energetic and dynamic seem to be popular words for describing the city of Barcelona. It's not only visual artists who work on the Ramblas and find inspiration in it; musicians, too, love the Ramblas. Some find it to be not only stimulating, but also a great source for contemporary international music and art trends. One musician explains what it's like to work and play here. 'It's a very nice place,' he says, 'because in the Ramblas you can find theatre, music from Argentina, from Spain, from Africa, from all [over] the world.'

The cultural mix of the area provides an exciting creative environment for the artists and entertainers from around the world. In one corner of the Ramblas, you can find beautifully dressed dancers performing a traditional Argentinean dance called the 'tango.' In another, you can find a small musical group **jamming**[6] and singing along to a catchy rock tune in English. It's obvious that artists of all types, nations, and genders **thrive**[7] in the atmosphere of improvisation and spontaneity.

---

[6]**jam:** (*slang*) take part in an impromptu musical performance
[7]**thrive:** do well

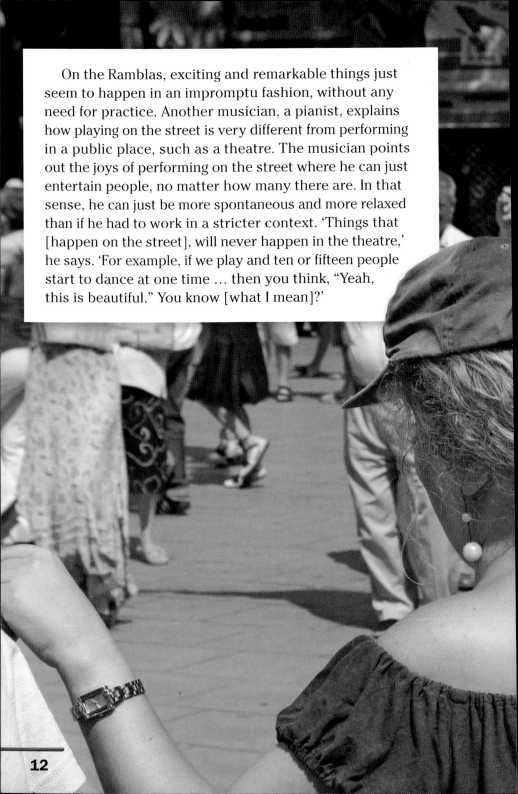

On the Ramblas, exciting and remarkable things just seem to happen in an impromptu fashion, without any need for practice. Another musician, a pianist, explains how playing on the street is very different from performing in a public place, such as a theatre. The musician points out the joys of performing on the street where he can just entertain people, no matter how many there are. In that sense, he can just be more spontaneous and more relaxed than if he had to work in a stricter context. 'Things that [happen on the street], will never happen in the theatre,' he says. 'For example, if we play and ten or fifteen people start to dance at one time ... then you think, "Yeah, this is beautiful." You know [what I mean]?'

Spontaneity, then, seems to be a predominant characteristic of Barcelona, and one of the reasons why people have so much **affection**[8] for the city. Perhaps another reason why people love life in this city is because some feel there is not such a separation between art and life. In Barcelona, it seems that the two have become **intertwined**[9] in a way that makes living here very entertaining.

The pianist then explains that entertainment is everywhere here, and that Barcelona is a centre for entertainment in Europe, perhaps even in the world. According to him, one can't escape entertainment In the city – it's all around: 'Ramblas is the street in Barcelona – and I think in Europe and maybe in the world – [where] you're going to be entertained – no matter how!'

It's not just singing and dancing that makes the city interesting, he adds, but it is the visual environment as well. He points out how artistically decorated things can be in the city right down to the flower shops. 'I mean if you walk past the flower shops,' he notes, 'the way they build [the flower arrangements] up is beautiful.' He then points out that the street itself is beautiful, as well. 'Even the street is decorated,' he explains, referring to the colourful **paving stones**[10] on some parts of the Ramblas. He then concludes by adding his view on visiting the city, 'I mean you get entertained. It's worth coming to Barcelona.'

---

[8]**affection:** a feeling close to love; warmth for something or someone
[9]**intertwine:** combine; mix
[10]**paving stone:** a flat piece of stone used to surface a walking area

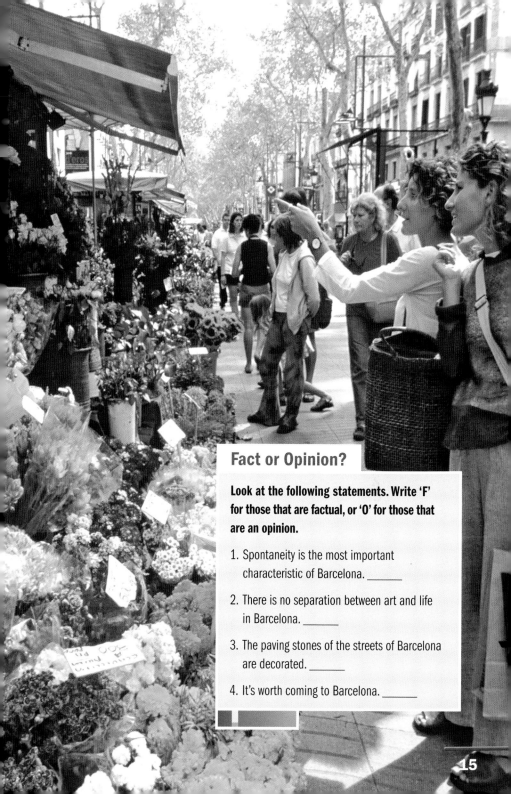

Fact or Opinion?

Look at the following statements. Write 'F' for those that are factual, or 'O' for those that are an opinion.

1. Spontaneity is the most important characteristic of Barcelona. _____

2. There is no separation between art and life in Barcelona. _____

3. The paving stones of the streets of Barcelona are decorated. _____

4. It's worth coming to Barcelona. _____

Although a variety of performers entertain in Barcelona, the city has become well-known for one particular type of entertainer. A common sight while walking along the Ramblas is a silver statue standing on a dais in the middle of the street, but these statues are different; they can reach out and touch you if they want. They are actually people dressed up to appear like statues. If a coin drops in front of them, they'll sometimes suddenly move, which can cause onlookers to jump away in surprise.

Human statues are a popular form of street entertainment which, although they're not exclusive to the city, have definitely been made famous in Barcelona. The artists' performances usually consist of a man or woman dressing up as a character and covering themselves in silver or gold make-up, but sometimes a performer likes to joke with the audience. He or she then stands very still, and suddenly moves when the perfect 'victim' comes too close. This often shocks the person and results in laughter from nearby spectators, who may have been wondering whether the statue was a performer or not!

One street performer who works as a statue takes a moment to talk about life as a street entertainer in Barcelona. 'I don't see myself as a statue,' he says as he relaxes in his silver gangster costume. 'I see myself more as a performer.' So how does he prepare for this interesting acting job? For him, it's just like any other job. He says: 'Preparation is waking up in the morning and putting on [my] clothes. There's nothing more to it. I sit down in front of a mirror. I get a little bit of make-up. I put it on my face. I put it in my hair, my hat, my suit. I have one look in front of the mirror, and then I **hit it**.'[11]

Later, the performer seems to sum up the attitude of many of the the artists and entertainers who work and play on the Ramblas. According to this artist, it's simply a way of life to perform on the streets of the city. 'It's a way of life,' he begins. '(On the) Ramblas … you have everything. You have traffic. You have people. You have tourists. You have thieves. You have performers. Ramblas has everything. It's a **vibrant**[12] life.' The performer then concludes, 'It's a way of life. It's truly a way of life.' Then he adds with a big smile, 'I love it!' The street performer is not the only one who loves the Ramblas; as one watches the crowds gather and the artists perform, it's easy to see how they could fall in love with this beautiful, vibrant city. The exciting streets of Barcelona make life *vital*!

---

[11] **hit it:** (*slang*) go; get started
[12] **vibrant:** full of life and energy

After You Read

1. The circus group mentioned in paragraph 2 on page 4 is given as an example of:
   A. an impromptu performance
   B. a party that never ends
   C. a typical group of jazz musicians
   D. a welcoming atmosphere

2. The word 'cuts' in paragraph 1 on page 7 can be replaced by:
   A. accesses
   B. locates
   C. runs
   D. occupies

3. Which of the following is a suitable headline for page 7?
   A. Spain's Dark Streets
   B. The Joys of Eating
   C. Spectators Sigh
   D. Any Age OK

4. Which country has the artist on page 8 visited?
   A. Germany
   B. The Netherlands
   C. Spain
   D. Amsterdam

5. What is 'it' in 'find inspiration in it' referring to on page 11?
   A. working
   B. music
   C. the Ramblas
   D. Barcelona

6. What is the purpose of page 11?
   A. to illustrate that performers come from all over the world
   B. to introduce a traditional Argentinean dance
   C. to list the kinds of performances that can be seen on the Ramblas
   D. to contrast South American dance with British rock

7. What point does the pianist make about performing on the Ramblas on page 12?
   A. He has to compete with a lot of other entertainers.
   B. He prefers to perform in a theatre.
   C. The public does not pay as much attention to street performers.
   D. The atmosphere encourages him to be creative.

8. The word 'predominant' on page 14 is closest in meaning to:
   A. traditional
   B. leading
   C. permanent
   D. casual

9. Barcelona's restaurants and food add to the unique atmosphere of the city.
   A. True
   B. False
   C. Not in text

10. Human statues are popular performers _____ they often shock people and make spectators laugh.
   A. where
   B. by
   C. which
   D. as

11. Which of the following sentences best expresses the meaning of the explanation about preparation on page 18?
   A. The routine must be done in a speedy fashion.
   B. Getting ready is comprised of many steps.
   C. Make-up takes time because it can fade easily.
   D. The process of preparation is quite simple.

12. It can be inferred that the writer thinks:
   A. Barcelona would be fun as a visitor but too noisy as a resident.
   B. Barcelona would be a great place to live.
   C. Most people in Barcelona are performers.
   D. Barcelona has more immigrants than residents.

10th of August

To the members of the city council of Albion,

As a lifelong resident of Albion I have seen many changes to our beautiful town. Fifty years ago, the population was 32,000 and Main Street was the centre of everything. People went there to shop, eat in restaurants, watch films and sometimes just walk around and visit with people. Today, Albion's population is over 80,000 and nobody even thinks about going to the city centre. We shop at shopping centres and on the Internet. We get take aways and stay at home and watch TV. Most of the city centre businesses have closed, putting people out of work, and taking away thousands of dollars of local tax revenue.

I advocate a radical proposal to turn things around. Let's declare the large area to the north of Main Street a pedestrian-only zone. Once we accomplish that, we can begin creating a lively street scene with antique stores, open-air markets, pavement cafés and street musicians or other performers. Instead of going to another city for entertainment, people may start making central Albion their free-time destination. Parents can bring their children, and teenagers would be able to get together in a safe, public setting. New public transport options could encourage people to leave their cars at home and provide the city with additional income.

The changes could also have economic benefits for the city. Art galleries, clothes shops, and other businesses might begin to convert the abandoned shops into new businesses, providing renewed visitor traffic. As city centre street life becomes more exciting, Main Street could also begin to attract new residents.

Statistics Before and After Institution of Car-Free Zone in Springfield, WA	Before 2003	After 2008
Average Weekly Restaurant Revenue	$28,000	$101,000
Percentage of Unoccupied Hotel Rooms	22%	7%
Public Transport Revenues	$43,500	$51,500
Business Tax Revenues	$85,000	$121,000
Council Tax Revenues	$56,000	$120,000
Unemployment	11%	4%
Total Road Traffic Accidents	8	3

Young people responding to the energising atmosphere may move into the flats above the shops. In this instance, property developers will start building new flats, providing new housing as well as work for local residents. All of this activity would help to restore the city's business and council tax base.

If you want confirmation that this kind of plan works, just look at Springfield's results. When they brought in their pedestrian-only zone in 2003, the changes were dramatic. Restaurants and hotels began to fill up, tax revenues rose, unemployment rates went down and there were even fewer road traffic accidents and deaths. At the same time, the people of the town gained an exciting new neighbourhood. I certainly hope you'll give this idea your serious consideration.

Yours sincerely,
Mary Beth Blakely

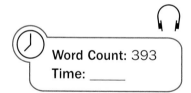

Word Count: 393
Time: _____

Vocabulary List

affection (14)
artistically (2, 4, 14)
boulevard (7)
dais (3, 17)
favourably (8)
gangster (3, 18)
hit it (18)
hub (7)
impromptu (4, 11, 12)
improvise (2, 4, 7, 11)
intertwine (14)
jam (11)
make-up (2, 3, 17, 18)
market stalls (3, 7)
onlooker (2, 3, 17)
paving stone (14)
pedestrian (2, 7)
spontaneous (2, 11, 12, 14)
stimulating (2, 11)
thrive (11)
vibrant (18)
vital (8, 18)